KANSAS

A MyReportLinks.com Book

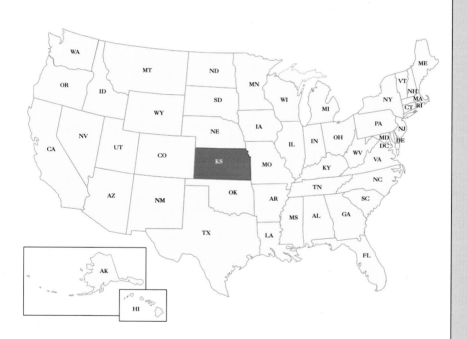

Jennifer Reed

MyReportLinks.com Books

an imprint of

Enslow Publishers, Inc.
Box 398, 40 Industrial Road
Berkeley Heights, NJ 07922
USA

To my parents for their kindness and Kansas spirit

MyReportLinks.com Books, an imprint of Enslow Publishers, Inc. MyReportLinks is a trademark of Enslow Publishers, Inc.

Library of Congress Cataloging-in-Publication Data

Reed, Jennifer.
  Kansas / Jennifer Bond Reed.
    p. cm. — (States)
Summary: Discusses the land and climate, economy, government, and history of the state of Kansas. Includes Internet links to Web sites.
Includes bibliographical references and index.
  ISBN 0-7660-5140-4
  1. Kansas—Juvenile literature. [1. Kansas.] I. Title. II. States
(Series : Berkeley Heights, N.J.)
  F681.3.R44 2003
  978.1—dc21
                              2002153560

Printed in the United States of America

10 9 8 7 6 5 4 3 2 1

To Our Readers:
Through the purchase of this book, you and your library gain access to the Report Links that specifically back up this book.
The Publisher will provide access to the Report Links that back up this book and will keep these Report Links up to date on **www.myreportlinks.com** for three years from the book's first publication date.
We have done our best to make sure all Internet addresses in this book were active and appropriate when we went to press. However, the author and the Publisher have no control over, and assume no liability for, the material available on those Internet sites or on other Web sites they may link to.
The usage of the MyReportLinks.com Books Web site is subject to the terms and conditions stated on the Usage Policy Statement on **www.myreportlinks.com**.
A password may be required to access the Report Links that back up this book. The password is found on the bottom of page 4 of this book.
Any comments or suggestions can be sent by e-mail to comments@myreportlinks.com or to the address on the back cover.

Photo Credits: ArtToday.com, pp. 22, 45; © Corel Corporation, pp. 3, 27; © Harland J. Schuster, pp. 11, 13, 14, 18, 20, 39, 41; © 2001 Robesus, Inc., p. 10 (flag); © 2003 Information of Kansas, Inc., pp. 29, 33; Dwight D. Eisenhower Library, p. 36; Enslow Publishers, Inc., pp. 1, 19; Erin Gerber/Washburn University, p. 35; Family of Amelia Earhart c/o CMG Worldwide, p. 16; Library of Congress, pp. 3 (Constitution), 24, 26; MyReportLinks.com Books, p. 4; National Archives, p. 31; PBS, p. 43; Ronald Reagan Library, p. 37.

Cover Photo: © Harland J. Schuster

Cover Description: The state capitol building in Topeka, Kansas, with a statue of Abraham Lincoln in front.

Contents

MyReportLinks.com Books
Great Books, Great Links, Great for Research!

MyReportLinks.com Books present the information you need to learn about your report subject. In addition, they show you where to go on the Internet for more information. The pre-evaluated Report Links that back up this book are kept up to date on **www.myreportlinks.com**. With the purchase of a MyReportLinks.com Books title, you and your library gain access to the Report Links that specifically back up that book. The Report Links save hours of research time and link to dozens—even hundreds—of Web sites, source documents, and photos related to your report topic.

Please see "To Our Readers" on the Copyright page for important information about this book, the MyReportLinks.com Books Web site, and the Report Links that back up this book.

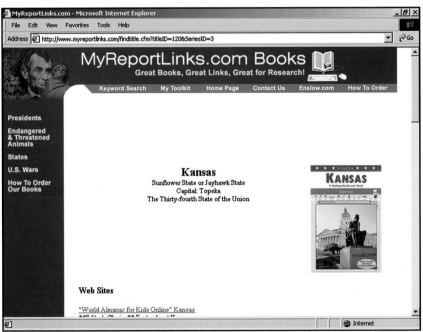

Access:

The Publisher will provide access to the Report Links that back up this book and will try to keep these Report Links up to date on our Web site for three years from the book's first publication date. Please enter **SKS7845** if asked for a password.

Report Links

 The Internet sites described below can be accessed at
http://www.myreportlinks.com

*EDITOR'S CHOICE

▶**The *World Almanac for Kids Online*: Kansas**
The *World Almanac for Kids Online* presents a vast collection of facts
about Kansas, including information about the state's land and
resources, population, education, culture, government, politics,
economy, and more.

Link to this Internet site from http://www.myreportlinks.com
*EDITOR'S CHOICE

▶**Today In History: Kansas**
On January 29, 1861, Kansas entered the Union. This Web site describes
that day, as well as Kansas' history prior to entering the Union.

Link to this Internet site from http://www.myreportlinks.com
*EDITOR'S CHOICE

▶**Explore the States: Kansas**
America's Story from America's Library, a Library of Congress Web site,
tells the story of Kansas including tales about a local band, a medicine
lodge, Strawberry Hill, "Little Sweden," and more.

Link to this Internet site from http://www.myreportlinks.com
*EDITOR'S CHOICE

▶**A Collection of Digitized Kansas Maps**
This Web site holds 325 digitized maps from 1556 to 1900. Each map is
described in detail and categorized by date.

Link to this Internet site from http://www.myreportlinks.com
*EDITOR'S CHOICE

▶**Kansas State Historical Society**
The Kansas State Historical Society Web site is an organization that
collects and produces vast amounts of research about the state.
You will find information about archeology, government, historic
properties, and much more.

Link to this Internet site from http://www.myreportlinks.com
*EDITOR'S CHOICE

▶**U.S. Census Bureau: Kansas**
The U.S. Census Bureau Web site provides facts and statistics about
the state's demographics, businesses, and geography.

Link to this Internet site from http://www.myreportlinks.com

Report Links

The Internet sites described below can be accessed at
http://www.myreportlinks.com

▶ **AccessKansas**

The state's official Web site provides a gateway to information about Kansas.
Here you will learn about Kansas' education, government, business, lifestyle,
labor, and recreation. You will also find a brief history and a list of facts.

Link to this Internet site from http://www.myreportlinks.com

▶ **An Act to Organize the Territories of Nebraska and Kansas**

From The Avalon Project at Yale Law School you can read and learn about the
Kansas-Nebraska Act.

Link to this Internet site from http://www.myreportlinks.com

▶ **Bleeding Kansas**

This Web site describes the period in Kansas' history known as Bleeding
Kansas. Here you will learn about how the Nebraska-Kansas Act caused a
violent outbreak between abolitionists and people who were pro slavery.

Link to this Internet site from http://www.myreportlinks.com

▶ **Infoplease.com: Kansas**

Infoplease.com provides a brief history of Kansas. You will also find
information about its government and famous people from the state.

Link to this Internet site from http://www.myreportlinks.com

▶ **John Brown's Holy War**

This Web site describes John Brown's controversial fight against slavery and
the Pottawatomie Massacre.

Link to this Internet site from http://www.myreportlinks.com

▶ **Kansas**

The NetState Web site provides information about Kansas: its symbols,
people, geography, history, and much more.

Link to this Internet site from http://www.myreportlinks.com

Report Links

↗ The Internet sites described below can be accessed at
http://www.myreportlinks.com

▶**Kansas Aviation Museum**
Kansans call Wichita the "Air Capital of the World," and this site captures that spirit. Included are narratives and photographs relating to historic sights and buildings that are now part of the Kansas Aviation Museum.

Link to this Internet site from http://www.myreportlinks.com

▶**The Kansas Barbed Wire Museum**
Barbed wire has a significant role in the history of the American prairie. This unique museum displays over one thousand varieties of barbed wire. Included is an extensive history of barbed wire and barbed wire collecting.

Link to this Internet site from http://www.myreportlinks.com

▶**Kansas Fruit Grower's Association**
The Kansas Fruit Grower's Association's official Web site provides comprehensive information on fruit growing in Kansas. You will also find a guide to the state's fruits and orchards, the history of fruit growing in Kansas, and a map that highlights major orchards and their produce.

Link to this Internet site from http://www.myreportlinks.com

▶**Kansas Heritage**
The Kansas Heritage Group archives are devoted to digitally preserving Kansas' past, and giving future generations the opportunity to learn about family and local history. A wide variety of relevant historical documents and data is also available.

Link to this Internet site from http://www.myreportlinks.com

▶**Kansas Photo Tour**
This unique site allows the visitor to join a virtual photographic tour of the entire state. You will find an index of sites and an interactive map that makes navigation easy.

Link to this Internet site from http://www.myreportlinks.com

▶**Kansas Sampler Foundation**
The Kansas Sampler Foundation Web site provides a gateway to the rural culture of Kansas. This foundation preserves and presents the state's architecture, art, commerce, cuisine, customs, geography, and history of its people.

Link to this Internet site from http://www.myreportlinks.com

Report Links

The Internet sites described below can be accessed at
http://www.myreportlinks.com

▶**Kansas Territory: Crucible of American Experience**
This Web site presents nineteenth-century Kansas history through
original manuscripts.

Link to this Internet site from http://www.myreportlinks.com

▶**Natural Kansas**
Natural Kansas is a wonderful interactive guide to the biological and
geological diversity of the state. Included are interactive maps, diagrams,
images, regional guides, and a bibliography.

Link to this Internet site from http://www.myreportlinks.com

▶**The Official Site of Amelia Earhart**
Born in Atchison, Kansas, Amelia Earhart was the first woman to fly solo
across the Atlantic. She also attempted to fly around the world. At this Web
site you can read about her life and career as an aviator.

Link to this Internet site from http://www.myreportlinks.com

▶**Perry-Castañeda Map Collection—Kansas**
The Perry-Castañeda Map Collection, administered by the University of Texas
at Austin, presents this collection of Kansas' state, city, and historic maps.
You will also find maps of Kansas' national parks and monuments.

Link to this Internet site from http://www.myreportlinks.com

▶**Stately Knowledge: Kansas**
The Stately Knowledge Web site provides a brief introduction to facts about
the state. You will also find links to other online resources about Kansas.

Link to this Internet site from http://www.myreportlinks.com

▶**Surviving the Dust Bowl**
This Web site describes the Dust Bowl years and the affect the Dust Bowl had
on people in places such as Texas, Oklahoma, Kansas, Colorado, and New
Mexico. Here you will find a time line of events, maps, and personal accounts.

Link to this Internet site from http://www.myreportlinks.com

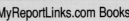

Report Links

 The Internet sites described below can be accessed at
http://www.myreportlinks.com

▶ **Susanna Madora Salter**
This Web site describes the story behind how Susanna Madora Salter
was the first woman ever to be elected mayor of Argonia, Kansas.

Link to this Internet site from http://www.myreportlinks.com

▶ **Today In History**
This site contains a brief biography of the author of *The Wonderful
Wizard of Oz* and literary criticism about the book.

Link to this Internet site from http://www.myreportlinks.com

▶ **Trip to North Western and West Central Kansas**
The Trip to North Western and West Central Kansas Web site explores
different places in Kansas. Here you will learn about Nicodemus,
Jennings, Monument Rocks, and Castle Rock.

Link to this Internet site from http://www.myreportlinks.com

▶ **Welcome to the Department of Wildlife and Parks**
The Department of Wildlife and Parks Web site offers information
about hunting, boating, fishing, state parks, and much more.

Link to this Internet site from http://www.myreportlinks.com

▶ **William F. Cody**
In 1857, William F. Cody, also known as Buffalo Bill, moved to Kansas
with his mother. At this Web site you can read about his life and how
he became a legend of the Wild West.

Link to this Internet site from http://www.myreportlinks.com

▶ *The Wizard of Oz:* **An American Fairy Tale**
Read about the adaptation of *The Wizard of Oz* from book, to stage, to
film. You will also find posters, movie stills, and other interesting pieces
of memorabilia.

Link to this Internet site from http://www.myreportlinks.com

▷ **Capital**
Topeka

▷ **Gained Statehood**
January 29, 1861,
the thirty-fourth state

▷ **Counties**
105

▷ **Population**
2,688,418*

▷ **Motto**
Ad astra per aspera
(Latin for "To the stars
through difficulties")

▷ **Nicknames**
Sunflower State
Jayhawk State

▷ **Tree**
Cottonwood

▷ **Flower**
Sunflower

▷ **Bird**
Western meadowlark

▷ **Animal**
American buffalo

▷ **Insect**
Honeybee

▷ **Reptile**
Ornate box turtle

▷ **Amphibian**
Barred tiger salamander

▷ **Song**
"Home on the Range" (words
by Brewster Higley, music by
Daniel Kelley)

▷ **Flag**
The state seal sits in the center
of a dark blue field. A sunflower
on a bar of twisted gold lies
above the seal. The word
"Kansas" lies below. The seal
shows a landscape under a rising
sun. A farmer is plowing a field
near his log cabin; a wagon train
is heading west; and buffalo
are fleeing from two American
Indians. Thirty-four stars ap-
pear above this scene showing
that Kansas is the thirty-fourth
state. Above the stars is the
state motto.

Population reflects the 2000 census.

Kansas and the Pioneer Spirit

When people think of Kansas, they often imagine flat, wide-open spaces that are full of wheat and populated with the descendants of pioneers. However, the landscape and people of Kansas are surprisingly varied. Each area has its own unique history, traditions, and culture.

▶ A Land of Nicknames

The official nickname for Kansas is the Sunflower State. In 1903, the sunflower was named the state flower. This bright yellow flower grows in Kansas fields and along the sides of roads.

Because of its central location in the United States, some people refer to the state

This wheat field in Brown County, in northeast Kansas, is ready for harvest. Most of the United States' cereals, breads, and grains are made from wheat grown in the state.

as *Midway, USA*. Another nickname is the *Wheat State*. Kansas is known for its wheat fields, and the huge amount of wheat it produces. Kansas has also been called the breadbasket of the world, because wheat grown in Kansas feeds many countries around the globe.

A fourth nickname is the *Jayhawk* or *Jayhawker State*. This comes from a term first used in present-day Kansas about 1858. Jayhawkers were the bands of raiders active along the Kansas-Missouri border before and during the Civil War, which ended in 1865. The name soon lost its negative aspect and people born in Kansas are sometimes called Jayhawkers. A Jayhawk is a combination of two birds—the blue jay, which enjoys squabbling, and the sparrow hawk, which is a fierce hunter. It is the school mascot of the University of Kansas, and is said to bring good luck to its sports teams.

Plains, Prairies, and History

Each year, Kansas attracts tourists from all over the world. It is a great state for sightseeing, hiking, biking, and other recreational activities. There are also many historic sites that allow visitors to relive life on the plains and prairies. They can learn the traditions of the American Indians, and explore parts of the Santa Fe and Oregon Trails.

Visitors looking for Wild West history can see old forts and cow towns, and explore a number of museums. The U.S. Cavalry Museum in Fort Riley tells the history of mounted soldiers from 1775 through 1950. The Hollenberg Station State Historic Site, near Hanover, gives a glimpse of the life of Pony Express riders and pioneers.

The southwestern portion of Kansas is where the Wild West began. The town of Dodge City is located here. For a time, it was known as "the wickedest little city in

▲ *This mural appears at the Pony Express station in Hanover, Kansas. The Hanover station is the only one that remains in its original form. The Pony Express, itself, was in business from April 1860 to November 1861.*

America." One cowboy wrote, "It were a sight to see: saloons, gambling houses, dance halls on every corner."[1] Visitors can stroll along the boardwalk in Old Dodge City, see reenactments of gunfights, and ride in stage-coaches. They can also pay a visit to Boot Hill Cemetery where many cowboys "died with their boots on."

The writer Laura Ingalls Wilder (1867–1957) described life in a one-room cabin and the landscape around her Kansas home in *The Little House on the Prairie*, published in 1935. The Ingalls family soon moved away from Kansas. Many years later, in the late 1970s, a replica of the cabin was built on the site where it once stood, near Independence. The Tallgrass Prairie National Reserve in

east-central Kansas was created to protect the grassland and the animals that live there. Prairie chickens and meadowlarks nest in the tall grasses. Badgers, foxes, deer, and bobcats also live on the prairie. This national park features a one-room schoolhouse and a nineteenth-century ranch.

Digging for fossils is a popular activity for visitors. In the high plains of northwestern Kansas are prairies and wheat fields that were under a deep sea millions of years ago. In this part of Kansas you can find fossils like sharks' teeth and dinosaur bones. There are good collections of fossils of dinosaurs, birds, mammals, reptiles, and invertebrates at the University of Kansas Natural History Museum in Lawrence, and at the Sternberg Museum of Natural History in Hays.

▲ Known as Monument Rocks, these limestone formations are located in Gove County, Kansas. They reach heights of sixty feet, but originally they were the floor of a vast, inland sea.

Some of the history in Kansas is more recent. The Kansas Cosmosphere and Space Center in Hutchinson is one of the Midwest's leading tourist attractions. Its Hall of Space Museum tells the story of the race to the moon. It also has a large collection of United States and Russian space items.

Other attractions in Kansas include the beautiful chalk pyramids called Monument Rocks. These unusual formations are found in the far western portion of the state. Some formations rise as high as sixty feet and are millions of years old. They were created when the sea that once covered Kansas receded. The pioneers used these rocks as landmarks.[2]

Born Pioneers

Many famous Americans were born in Kansas or spent much of their lives there. Early figures include the frontiersman and marshal "Wild Bill" Hickok (1837–76) and Wild West personality "Buffalo Bill" Cody (1846–1917). Cody moved to Kansas as a child and grew up on a farm near Leavenworth, Kansas. Carry A. Nation (1846–1911), a crusader against alcohol, spent much of her adult life in Kansas.

Many poets, authors, artists, and entertainers enjoyed the beauty of the land and perhaps gained inspiration from the pioneer spirit. Poet Gwendolyn Brooks (1917–2000) was born in Topeka, as was Harlem Renaissance artist and illustrator Aaron Douglas (1899–1979). Dorothy Canfield Fisher (1879–1958) was born in Lawrence. She is best known for writing books for children and young adults. Playwright William Inge (1913–73) was born in Independence and educated at the University of Kansas. He wrote *Picnic* (1953) and

Bus Stop (1955). Jazz saxophone player Charlie "Bird" Parker (1920–55) was born in Kansas City. A couple of well-known actors are from Kansas as well. Hattie McDaniel (1895–1952) was famous for her role as the faithful slave Mammy in the movie *Gone With the Wind*, which hit screens in 1939. Actor and comedian Buster Keaton (1895–1966) was born in Piqua, Kansas.

Many well-known politicians have called Kansas home. President Dwight D. Eisenhower (1890–1969) was born in Texas, but moved to Abilene, Kansas, at a very young age. Former senator and presidential candidate Robert "Bob" Dole (1923–) is a native of Russell, Kansas.

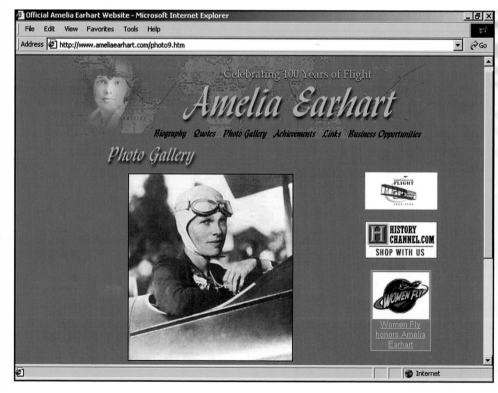

▲ Once Amelia Earhart decided she wanted to fly, she was determined to overcome financial obstacles and break social bounds. In 1928, she was the first woman to fly solo across the United States.

Nancy Kassebaum was a United States senator 1979 to 1997. Senator Kassebaum's father was Alf Landon. He was governor of Kansas from 1932 to 1937, and ran for president in 1936.

Kansas was also the birthplace of a number of great athletes. Among them was former heavyweight champion Jess Willard, who held the title in 1915. Baseball Hall of Famers Joe Tinker (1880–1948) and Walter "Big Train" Johnson (1887–1946) were also born in Kansas. Runner Jim Ryun, from Wichita, Kansas, won a silver medal at the 1968 Olympics. He later turned to politics, and was first elected as a Kansas member of the U.S. House of Representatives in 1996. Legendary football running backs Barry Sanders and Gale Sayers also hailed from the state. Sayers was known as the Kansas Comet.

Amelia Earhart is one of the most famous Kansans. She was born in 1897 and was the first woman to fly solo across the Atlantic. In 1937, she attempted to fly around the world. Sadly, her plane disappeared over the Pacific Ocean.

Another name well-known in the transportation industry is that of automaker Walter Chrysler, born in Wamego in 1875. At the time Chrysler retired in 1935 his Chrysler Corporation was the second largest automobile maker in the world.

Chapter 2 ▶

Land and Climate

Kansas covers 82,282 square miles in the western part of the central United States. Most people consider it to be a Midwestern state. It is nearly rectangular and is more than four hundred miles wide and two hundred miles from north to south. It is surrounded by four states: Nebraska lies to the north, Missouri to the east, Oklahoma to the south, and Colorado to the west.

Kansas is part of two natural regions in the United States—the Central Lowlands and the Great Plains. The landscape is more varied and less flat than people think. The land climbs from an elevation of 680 feet in the southeastern

◀ *Mt. Sunflower is the highest point in Kansas. People come to this spot to relax, listen to the wind, and enjoy the vast prairie.*

▲ A map of Kansas

corner to its highest point, 4,039 feet at Mount Sunflower on the western border.

▶ Geographic Regions

Kansas is divided into four main regions from west to east: The High Plains, Plains Border, the Southeastern Plains, and the Dissected Till Plains. The High Plains and Plains Border areas are part of the Great Plains, which cover the center of the United States. The Dissected Till Plains and the Southeastern Plains cover the eastern third of the state and are part of the Central Lowlands.

Valleys and canyons run through the gently rolling land of the High Plains. There are few trees in this relatively high section of Kansas. Many prehistoric fossils of fish and other sea creatures have been found here. Fossils

of flying reptiles can be found at the Fick Fossil Museum and History Museum in Oakley, along with more than ten thousand petrified shark teeth. It seems strange, but sharks once swam freely over the area we know as Kansas.

The Plains Border region is located in the middle third of the state, and is the transitional zone between the Central Lowlands and the High Plains. The Smoky Hills and Blue Hills are found here. This region is quite sandy, with dunes, hills, unusual rock formations, and chalk beds.

The Dissected Till Plains lie in the northeastern part of the state. This region was covered by glaciers in the Ice

▲ *The Big Basin Prairie Preserve is located in Clark County, Kansas. In the preserve are bison, midgrass prairies, and fossils.*

Tools   Search   Notes   Discuss   Go!

Age, and the landscape shows the effects of this. It has gentle, rolling hills, wide valleys, and many streams and rivers. The Missouri River runs along the northeast border of this region, and the Kansas River flows west to east across it.

South of the Dissected Till Plains are the Southeastern Plains, also known as the Osage Plains. This region includes an area called the Flint Hills that stretches south into Oklahoma. These hills are actually made mostly of limestone and offer some of the best grazing land in Kansas. The Ozark Mountains jut into the far southeastern portion of Kansas. Here, the land is hilly with winding rivers and dense forests.

Grassland

The land in Kansas is mostly covered with prairie. Almost two hundred types of grass grow in the state including, bluestem, prairie beardgrass, and turkeyfoot. The grasses in the western part of the state are much shorter than those that grow in the eastern section.

The prairies support Kansas's huge livestock industry. Cattle and bison graze in the grasslands. In 1997, the Tallgrass Prairie National Reserve was created to protect Kansas' grassland.

Climate

In general, the state enjoys a moderate climate, with an average annual temperature of 55°F. A record high temperature of 121°F was logged on July 18, 1936, in Fredonia, Kansas. The lowest temperature recorded was −40°F. These, though, are extremes. On average, summer temperatures hover around 78°F and winter temperatures around 30°F.

The western third of Kansas, the High Plains area, is very dry, has few trees, and receives the most sunshine. The eastern third of the state has more rainfall—an average of thirty-five inches per year. It is also more humid and has less sunshine.

The Kansas River was named for the Kansa people. *Kansa* means "people of the south wind." Kansas is the fourth-windiest state in the country. Only Massachusetts, Montana, and Wyoming experience more wind. Dodge City is the windiest city in the United States.

Unusual weather conditions can be created when hot, dry air masses come up from Mexico or frigid polar blasts blow down from the north. The sun, however, usually shines more than 275 days a year.

▶ Wild Weather

The weather can be extreme in any part of the state. Winter blizzards drop many feet of snow. Flooding and tornadoes are other threats to property, livestock,

◀ *Kansas' flat prairie landscape is the perfect haven for dust storms or tornadoes. An average of thirty-nine tornadoes strike Kansas each year.*

and residents. On average, there are thirty-nine tornadoes a year that touch down in Kansas. They usually occur in the Spring. Hailstorms also wreak havoc on the land and its people. The largest hailstone ever found was in Kansas. It measured 17 inches around. Hail destroys crops and can kill small animals.

▷ Water Problems

The amount of rainfall in Kansas can vary dramatically from year to year. Heavy rains some years lead to flooding, but in other years drought can threaten livestock and crops. In times of drought, the high winds pick up the dry top layers of soil and blow them through the air.

Huge dust storms in the 1930s blackened the skies in the middle of the day and devastated the land. The state became known as the Dust Bowl State.

A huge area of water-holding rock called the Ogallala aquifer lies underneath the western third of Kansas. This aquifer provides water for crops, and urban areas in Kansas and seven other states. However, the water level in this important source is dropping. Reasons for this include irrigation of fields and the demands of an increasing population. Kansans are now being careful with the amount of water they use.

Chapter 3

Economy

Kansas is rich in natural resources that make its economy strong. Agriculture was the main economic activity in Kansas until the middle of the twentieth century. Since then, manufacturing and service industries have grown in the state, and transportation has become an important contributor to the state's wealth.

▷ Agriculture

Much of Kansas lies on fertile land that is suited to growing a number of crops. Kansas is one of the most important

△ Toward the end of the 1800s, more and more railroads began to cross Kansas. This helped boost the shipment of wheat and livestock. Shown here is part of the Santa Fe Railroad in Argentine, Kansas.

agricultural states in the nation. The state also sells its agricultural products to countries around the world. Wheat, corn, sorghum, soybeans, and sunflowers are the most important crops. Kansas grows so much wheat that half of the wheat crop is exported.[1] Sorghum is used mostly as feed for livestock.

The extensive grasslands make Kansas an ideal place to raise beef cattle. Kansas farmers also raise dairy cattle, sheep, and, in the northeastern part of the state, hogs and poultry. Livestock and livestock products are the most important source of income for farmers.

Mining

Mining of natural resources was developed in Kansas in the early twentieth century. Today, it plays a smaller but still important role in the state's economy. Kansas is one of the top ten mineral-producing states. The main products are oil, natural gas, coal, salt, and stone. The natural gas also contains Helium.

The largest salt mine in Kansas is located in the town of Hutchinson. It is 650 feet deep. After the salt is removed from the underground vaults, these vast caves are then transformed into storage areas. The temperature and humidity make them perfect for keeping important items such as papers and film—including the original negative of *The Wizard of Oz*.

Transportation

Kansas has always attracted people interested in aviation, and Kansans have been building planes since as early as 1908. The vast countryside with few trees was an ideal place to test planes and experiment with flight. An anonymous person once said that "Kansas sometimes seems to

http://www.loc.gov/exhibits/oz/images/vc57.jpg - Microsoft Internet Explorer

File Edit View Favorites Tools Help

Address http://www.loc.gov/exhibits/oz/images/vc57.jpg

Let's go "OVER THE RAINBOW" with Judy in her greatest hit!

M-G-M
THE WIZARD OF OZ
starring
JUDY GARLAND

COLOR BY TECHNICOLOR

Frank Morgan · Ray Bolger · Bert Lahr · Jack Haley
Billie Burke · Margaret Hamilton · Charley Grapewin · And The Munchkins
A Victor Fleming Production

Directed by Victor Fleming · Produced by Mervyn LeRoy
A Metro-Goldwyn-Mayer Masterpiece Reprint

Done   Internet

▲ *Kansas is often associated with the story of* The Wizard of Oz. *The original novel was adapted into one of the most popular movies of all time.*

have more sky than ground. . . . So much sky that it almost seems to invite dreamers and explorers to test the limits."[3]

On April 8, 1920, a Laird Swallow, the first commercially produced airplane in the United States, made its first flight over Wichita, Kansas. Since then, Kansas has developed into the Air Capital of the World. Industry leaders such as Boeing, Cessna, Bombardier/Learjet, and Raytheon/Beech employ more than thirty-five thousand people in the area. Boeing is the largest aerospace manufacturer in the world. Its headquarters are in Seattle,

Washington, but Boeing has built airplanes in Kansas for decades.

Each year, Kansas produces about 60 percent of the western world's general aviation aircraft. Wichita is the leader in the production of military and business planes, and more private airplanes are produced there than any-where else in the nation.

▷ Other Industries

There are other major companies in Kansas in addition to aircraft manufacturers. Coleman Company sells its famous coolers and camping equipment. It started in 1900 when it rented oil lamps to miners. By the end of

▲ *The Boeing 707 was the first long range and high passenger capacity aircraft. The Boeing 707 AWACS (Airborne warning and control system aircraft), pictured here, was built for the United States Air Force.*

the twentieth century, Coleman became one of the most well known brands of coolers in the world.

Two college-aged brothers, Dan and Frank Carney, started their first restaurant in Wichita in 1958. To help set up the business, they borrowed six hundred dollars from their mother. The company they started, Pizza Hut, has now become one of the largest pizza delivery companies with franchises all over the world.

In 1968, Hillsboro Industries, Inc., a leading manufacturer of flatbeds and aluminum trailers, was founded in Hillsboro, Kansas. The company was started by two local businessmen who wanted to produce unique products. Great Plains ventures purchased the company in 1978.[4]

Sprint began as a small telephone company in Abilene, Kansas. They became an industry leader in long distance and mobile phone technology. The Hallmark greeting card company has its headquarters in Kansas as well. In addition, the state is known for railroads, hospitals, food preparation plants, and car manufacturers. The variety of industries in the state shows that there is a lot more going on in Kansas than just farmers growing wheat.

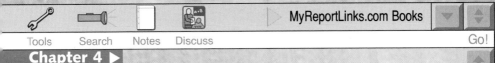

Government

Although Kansas has had a reputation of being a wild
place to live, Kansans have always agreed that there should
be law and order and a form of government. Before
Kansas became a state on January 29, 1861, the territory
of Kansas had a constitution that set out to protect the
rights of its citizens and provide for the common good.

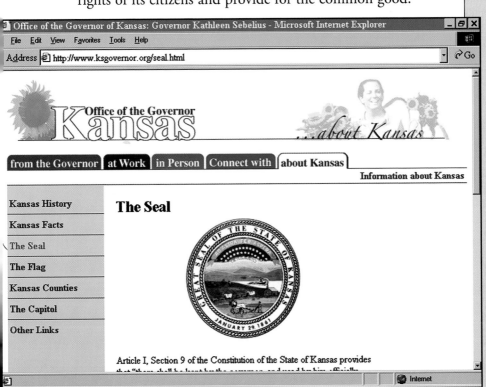

Office of the Governor of Kansas: Governor Kathleen Sebelius - Microsoft Internet Explorer

File   Edit   View   Favorites   Tools   Help

Address http://www.ksgovernor.org/seal.html   Go

Office of the Governor
Kansas   *...about Kansas*

from the Governor | at Work | in Person | Connect with | about Kansas

Information about Kansas

Kansas History

Kansas Facts

The Seal

The Flag

Kansas Counties

The Capitol

Other Links

The Seal

Article I, Section 9 of the Constitution of the State of Kansas provides

Internet

▲ Kansas's state constitution called for a state seal to "be kept by the
governor, and used by him officially." The seal depicts a scene along a
wagon trail, the state motto, and the date Kansas officially became a state.

Statehood

Kansas entered the Union as a free state and became the thirty-fourth state. However, statehood did not come easy. The decade before the Civil War was bloody, as people fought over whether or not Kansas should join the union as a free state or a slave state. Speaker of the House of Representatives, Henry Clay, proposed the Missouri Compromise in 1820. This compromise was to keep a balance between the states. It said that all territories north of Missouri's southern border would be free of slavery. States below would be slave states. Under those guidelines, Kansas would be a free state. However, many residents of the Kansas Territory wanted to own slaves.

Changes on the Horizon

Congress cancelled the Missouri Compromise with the new Kansas-Nebraska Act of 1854. This act gave residents of each territory the right to decide whether they would enter the Union as a slave state or free state. At the time, Congress had as many northern supporters as southern. When it came time to decide whether or not Kansas would be a free or slave state, the vote always ended in deadlock. Each side wanted Kansas to vote with them. At this time, Kansas' history was full of bloodshed and turmoil and the state became known as Bleeding Kansas.

First Elections

The first elections for the Kansas territorial legislature were held on March 30, 1855. On election day, several thousand pro slavery men known as Border Ruffians crossed into Kansas and voted illegally. They bullied voters and tried to intimidate election judges. It worked.

They defeated antislavery supporters and a pro slavery legislature was enacted. The constitution of the territory of Kansas was pro slavery and strong in its views. Fortunately, Congress had to approve this new territorial constitution and quickly rejected it.[1]

Antislavery settlers began the Free State Party. They held their own convention in Topeka in October 1855. They also created their own constitution. This constitution banned slavery. The following year, they elected their own governor and legislature. This too was rejected by Congress.

▲ This mural, by John Stewart Curry, The Tragic Prelude: John Brown, depicts this militant abolitionist. Brown led a group that killed five men at Pottawatomie Creek, Kansas. The mural is on display in the state capitol in Topeka.

▷ Bleeding Kansas

Pro slavery supporters called Bushwackers crossed the southern borders into the Kansas territory and illegally voted for pro slavery laws. Antislavery abolitionists called Jayhawks fought back. When other abolitionists heard of this, hundreds came from other territories and states to fight back. Finally, after a lot of fighting and violence Kansas entered the Union as a free state. Although, the violence did not end here. The Civil War started two months later. William Quantrill, a Kansas resident, wanted the state to be pro slavery. He joined the Confederate Army in Missouri and terrorized Kansans. His band was known as Quantrill's Raiders or The Wild Bunch.

Other well-known members of this group included Cole Younger and Frank and Jesse James. They committed one of the largest civilian massacres on August 21, 1863, when they invaded the town of Lawrence. They killed 150 men and burned over 200 homes and businesses to the ground.

The Bushwackers were not the only local terrorists in Kansas. Although antislavery abolitionists were generally peaceful, John Brown, the leader of the Jayhawks retaliated for the devastation in Lawrence. Brown and his supporters captured five pro slavery settlers from their cabins along the Pottawatomie Creek and killed them with swords. This happened just three days after Quantrill's massacre. Brown's attack became known as the Pottawatomie Massacre and because of this, Brown became a hero to many antislavery fanatics.

The Kansas Territory became a war zone for a couple of years between 1856 and 1858. Three attempts to draw up a state constitution failed. Finally, in July 1859 a new

Tools Search Notes Discuss Go!

state constitution was drawn up at a convention in Wyandotte. This is now a part of Kansas City, Kansas. It prohibited slavery much to the delight of abolitionists. Voters approved the new constitution and so did Congress. Topeka became, and still is, the capitol of Kansas.

Kansas Government

The Kansas state constitution is similar to the United States Constitution. It divides the government into three branches: executive, legislative, and judicial. A fine balance must be in place at both the federal level and the state level so that one branch of government does not have more power over the other.

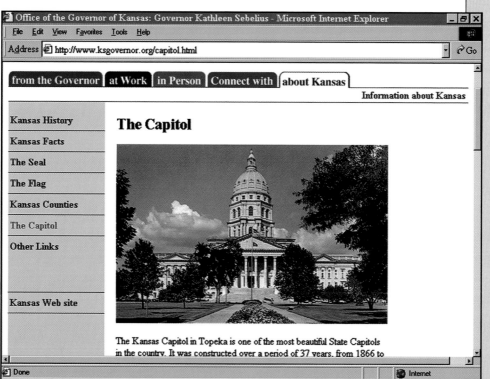

Office of the Governor of Kansas: Governor Kathleen Sebelius - Microsoft Internet Explorer

File Edit View Favorites Tools Help

Address http://www.ksgovernor.org/capitol.html

from the Governor | at Work | in Person | Connect with | about Kansas

Information about Kansas

Kansas History
Kansas Facts
The Seal
The Flag
Kansas Counties
The Capitol
Other Links

Kansas Web site

The Capitol

The Kansas Capitol in Topeka is one of the most beautiful State Capitols in the country. It was constructed over a period of 37 years, from 1866 to

Done   Internet

△ Topeka has been the state capital since Kansas entered the Union in 1861. The state capitol building, shown here, was completed in 1903.

The executive branch is led by the governor, who is the head of the state of Kansas. The governor prepares the budget and approves or rejects laws. Other elected officials of the executive branch include the lieutenant governor, the secretary of state, and the attorney general. All serve four-year terms.

The Kansas legislature is made up of a house of representatives and a senate. The house has 125 members elected for a two-year term and the state senate has 40 members elected to four-year terms. Once members of both houses approve a proposed law or bill it is sent to the governor.

The Kansas judicial branch is divided into the state supreme court, court of appeals, district courts and municipal courts. The supreme court is the state's highest court. There are seven supreme court justices who have authority over all the other courts. The governor selects the justices from a list of nominees. All judges, no matter what their jurisdiction, have the same duty; to interpret the laws made by the legislature and apply the laws fairly.

Kansas has 105 counties with thousands of cities and towns.[2] Within these cities and towns are local governments. They are an extended part of the state and federal governments. When the national government was formed, the designers of the constitution did not provide for local governments. Instead, they left this up to each state. Voters elect county officials including commissioners, the county sheriff, county treasurer, and clerk. Each town has its own mayor, council members, and town clerk, who are elected by the residents.

▶ "Firsts" in Kansas

Kansas is home to many independent thinkers and Susanna Madora Salter is one example. In 1887, long

before the rest of the nation, Kansas' men gave rights to Kansas' women. They agreed that women could vote in local elections. As a result, women in Argonia, Kansas, voted and elected Susanna Madora Salter to be the first woman mayor in the country.

Women have played an important role in Kansas's politics. Other firsts include Minnie Grinstead who, in 1918, was the first woman elected to the Kansas legislature. In 1932, Kathryn O'Loughlin was the first woman elected to the U.S. House of Representatives, and in 1949, Georgia Neese Clark Gray was the first woman appointed

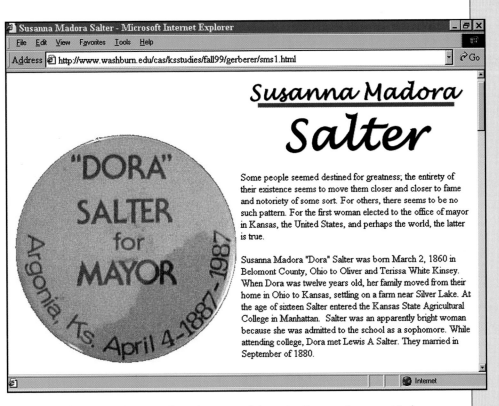

When she was elected mayor of Argonia, Kansas, Susanna Madora Salter was the first woman to be elected to this position in the United States. Shown here is a button commemorating the one hundredth anniversary of her election.

secretary of the U.S. Treasury. Finally in 1978, Nancy Landon Kassebaum was the first woman elected to represent the U.S. Senate.

Kansas was also the first state in the Union to ratify the Fifteenth Amendment to the Constitution, which granted voting rights to any American man, regardless of color.

Other Kansas Leaders

Perhaps it is the pioneer spirit that has rubbed off on so many independent thinkers and achievers in Kansas. This state has produced many firsts from Amelia Earhart, Clyde Cessna, to Susanna Madora Salter as well as well-known politicians such Dwight E. Eisenhower and Robert Dole.

Presidents Dwight E. Eisenhower excelled at high school sports in Abilene, Kansas. Accepted to the prestigious West Point Military Academy, Eisenhower rose to the top of his class. After graduation, he became a war hero for leading Allied troops to

Born in Texas, Dwight D. Eisenhower's family moved to Abilene, Kansas, while he was very young. A World War II hero, Eisenhower was elected president in 1952.

△ *Senator Bob Dole and his wife Elizabeth speak with President Ronald Reagan. Elizabeth Dole was President Reagan's Secretary of Transportation.*

victory in World War II, and for planning the successful D-day invasion. He proved himself a strong leader and was very popular. In 1952, he ran for president of the United States and won. The slogan that ran rampant across the Kansas prairies was "I like Ike!" He won his presidency and became the thirty-fourth president of the thirty-fourth state.

Robert Dole has also made Kansan's proud. He ran for the presidency in 1996. Although he lost to Bill Clinton, Dole will be remembered for serving Kansas, and the nation, well during his tenure in the U.S. Senate and the House of Representatives.

Chapter 5

History

Over fifteen thousand years ago, Paleo Indians roamed the plains of Kansas. They lived at the same time as the woolly mammoth. It is believed that this group of people originally came from Asia by crossing over a land bridge that once existed. It was located between what is now Alaska and Asia. Eventually, the Paleo Indians made their way to the western part of the United States and east to the Midwest. These people were nomadic, which meant they traveled from place to place in search of food. They followed the herds of mammoth and bison around the Great Plains. Where the food went, they went as well.

After the Paleo Indians came the Mound Builders. They buried their dead in large mounds, which are still found today. The biggest difference between the two groups of people is that the Mound Builders developed permanent villages. Kansas was an ideal place to live. The prairies were rich with bison, and the soil was perfect for growing crops. The many rivers and streams provided ample water. These natives realized the soil was good for planting. Corn and squash were grown. They made pottery, and used tools. The American Indians lived peacefully off the bounty of the land for thousands of years.

European explorers soon sailed to the Americas—what they called the New World. This "new world" was considered the land of plenty. The explorers were in search of vast riches, mainly gold. One Spanish explorer, Francisco Vásquez de Coronado heard of a city full of gold. It was called Quivira, and supposedly trees were hung with golden bells. Coronado was in Mexico when he began his journey in 1541, eighty years before the Pilgrims landed at Plymouth. With an American Indian guide that he called The Turk, who had been captured and enslaved, Coronado set off toward Kansas. The Turk wanted to find his home and rejoin his tribe, so he misled Coronado onward always telling him about the riches he would soon find. When Coronado reached Kansas he found grass huts and the Wichita Indians of the Quivira Tribe, but no city of gold. The Turk confessed that he had deceived the Spanish explorer and Coronado returned to the territory of New Mexico. Coronado was the first European traveler to set foot in Kansas.

Many American Indian tribes moved into the territory of Kansas by the 1500s. The Wichita and Pawnee both

△ Named after the famous Spanish explorer, Coronado Heights is located in the Smoky Hills. Some say that Coronado's men built this shelter in 1541 while digging for gold, but this is disputed.

lived here. The men hunted bison while the women tended to the crops. They lived in teepees made of bison skin. As more explorers ventured into the Kansas territory, the peaceful lives these Indians once led were soon to change.

In 1673, French explorers from Canada made their way to Kansas. They were not interested in gold, but wanted to trade furs. They found ample supplies of bison and beaver and began trading with the Osage and Pawnee Indians. The French thought they had discovered the land where Kansas is now located. Spain was sure they held the original claims to the land. As a result, France and Spain fought for the next hundred years over the land. This finally came to an end in 1803, when Thomas Jefferson persuaded France to sell to the United States its land west of the Mississippi River. This land deal was known as the Louisiana Purchase.

Kansas was named after the Kansa American Indian tribe. For thousands of years, the American Indians of Kansas lived freely and peacefully until European explorers and settlers moved in. In 1873, they were forced onto an Indian Reservation. Although Kansas is rich in American Indian history, the Indians of the Plains barely survived.

▷ Corps of Discovery

Kansas was the true frontier. Many people felt Kansas was the West. Thomas Jefferson had other ideas. He was fascinated with the land and all it had to offer. In 1804, Jefferson established the Corps of Discovery. Leading this group were Meriwether Lewis and William Clark. The Corps set out on the now famous Lewis and Clark Expedition. They were to journey across the land until they reached the Pacific Ocean and gather information about the land as they went. At this time, the Great Plains were believed to be unfit for cultivation. The area was nicknamed the Great American Desert.

As people on the East Coast demanded more land, they pushed the American Indians out and designated Kansas as a good place to put them. In 1830, Congress passed the Indian Removal Act, and made the Kansas Territory the permanent American Indian land. Thousands of American Indians were uprooted from their homes and sent to Kansas to live on reservations. Through this process, many lost their lives and were separated from their families.

▷ Rush for Gold

Soon word hit the east that there was gold in the west. Thousands of Easterners, mostly whites, packed up

△ *Oregon Trail Nature Park is located in Belvue, Kansas, 25 miles west of Topeka. Visitors can hike walking trails following part of the former Oregon Trail.*

their belongings and headed west hoping to gain success. Major trails leading to the far west passed through Kansas and made this territory a good stopping place. Miners and settlers traveled on the Overland Trail, the Oregon Trail, and the Santa Fe Trail to reach their final destinations. Small towns popped up all over the area as many people decided to settle there. The soil was rich and good for growing, and there were lots of bison that could be hunted for food and clothing. Suddenly, the whites, who sent the American Indians to live in Kansas, decided they wanted to live there, too. In 1854, the United States Congress opened the Kansas Territory up to homesteading and let the whites settle, even if it meant they would take over the American Indians' lands once again.

Years of violence occurred not only between the white settlers and American Indians, but also between whites and blacks, and between those who wanted a free state and those who wanted a slave state. These years leading up to the Civil War were full of bloodshed and rivalry. Bleeding Kansas was not a safe place to raise a family.

The Wild West

In the 1860s, drastic changes occurred in Kansas. Railroads developed which brought more white settlers to the area. The bison were the first to suffer. Men like "Buffalo" Bill Cody were hired to kill the bison to feed the railroad workers. Soon this became a sport, as people on trains would shoot bison for fun while the train rumbled across the Great Plains. By 1890, bison were nearly extinct from this excessive and unnecessary killing. Without bison, the American Indians who used them for food began to starve.

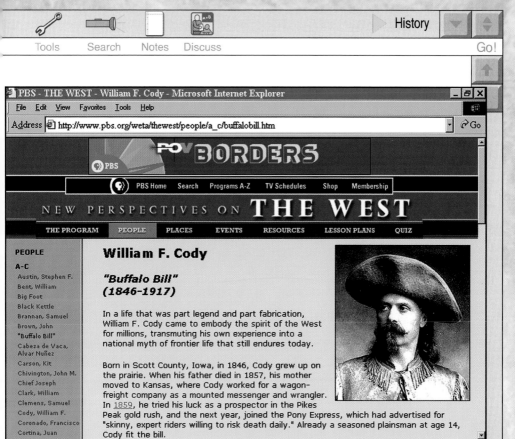

BORDERS

PBS

PBS Home   Search   Programs A-Z   TV Schedules   Shop   Membership

NEW PERSPECTIVES ON THE WEST

THE PROGRAM | PEOPLE | PLACES | EVENTS | RESOURCES | LESSON PLANS | QUIZ

PEOPLE

A-C

Austin, Stephen F.
Bent, William
Big Foot
Black Kettle
Brannan, Samuel
Brown, John
"Buffalo Bill"
Cabeza de Vaca, Alvar Nuñez
Carson, Kit
Chivington, John M.
Chief Joseph
Clark, William
Clemens, Samuel
Cody, William F.
Coronado, Francisco
Cortina, Juan

William F. Cody

"Buffalo Bill"
(1846–1917)

In a life that was part legend and part fabrication, William F. Cody came to embody the spirit of the West for millions, transmuting his own experience into a national myth of frontier life that still endures today.

Born in Scott County, Iowa, in 1846, Cody grew up on the prairie. When his father died in 1857, his mother moved to Kansas, where Cody worked for a wagon-freight company as a mounted messenger and wrangler. In 1859, he tried his luck as a prospector in the Pikes Peak gold rush, and the next year, joined the Pony Express, which had advertised for "skinny, expert riders willing to risk death daily." Already a seasoned plainsman at age 14, Cody fit the bill.

Internet

▲ William F. Cody, otherwise known as Buffalo Bill, spent much of his life in Kansas. He earned his nickname by shooting buffalo to feed the construction crews of the Kansas Pacific Railroad.

▶ Cowboys and Cow Towns

Cattle was abundant in Texas and soon cowboys drove their herds north to Kansas to cities such as Abilene, Dodge City, Wichita, and Ellsworth. They rode along the Chisholm, Western, and Shawnee Trails. The life of a cowboy was lonely and hard. When they sold their cattle in one of these towns, they made money and celebrated. The combination of money and alcohol made for some wild cowboys. Soon there were laws established to protect the people and maintain peace. Gunfighters and

lawmen became well known. One of the most famous lawmen was Wild Bill Hickok, whose real name was James Butler. He was the Marshal of Abilene in 1871 and became well known for controlling the unruly cowboys that frequented his town. Other famous Kansan lawmen include Wyatt Earp, Bat Masterson, and Doc Holliday.

▷ A Change for Kansas

As the era of cowboys died and industry grew, Kansans focused more on technology and ingenuity than on herding cattle. The Mennonites, a religious group from Russia brought with them a new variety of wheat called Turkey Red. This wheat grew well in Kansas. Production increased and new technologies were developed to grow large amounts of wheat.

By 1890, over a million people lived in Kansas.[1] After 1915, trucks, combines, and tractors replaced horses and plows. In addition, electricity was reaching rural areas and of course, the car was becoming less of a luxury and more of a necessity.

The Dust Bowl years of the 1930s drained the Kansas economy because the farmers could not grow many crops. The Dust Bowl was the result of drought and poor farming methods. Wind swept up a great layer of dust that blanketed almost the entire Midwest. Like the rest of the country, though, Kansas soon recovered. With World War II in 1941 and the popularity of Dwight D. Eisenhower, Kansans became more positive and had a renewed hope. Dams were built to prevent floods, agricultural methods were being developed and music and theatre were blossoming.

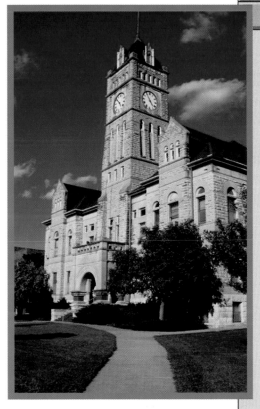

An image of the Atchison County Courthouse, located in Atchison, Kansas. The Courthouse was built by George P. Washburn, one of the most prominent architects of the nineteenth century.

Recent History

After World War II, the economy only got better. Families built homes, and cities grew into what they are today. Wheat, oil, and cattle, are still prominent in Kansas' economy. In the 1960s, farmers in Kansas and across the nation used new irrigation techniques to aid them in case of droughts.

This is not to say that Kansans are not faced with problems. Tornadoes and floods still plague the area at times, and droughts hurt farmers. Whatever the problems, though, a Kansan's spirit is tough. Just as tough as it was centuries ago.

Chapter 1. Kansas and the Pioneer Spirit

1. Don Worcester, *The Chisholm Trail: High Road of the Cattle Kingdom* (New York: Indian Head Books, 1994), p. 127.

2. John Hanna, "Monuments tower above rolling prairie," *The Keystone Gallery Home Page*, September 28, 1998, <http://www.keystonegallery.com/rockarticle.htm> (February 3, 2003).

Chapter 3. Economy

1. "Facts About Kansas Wheat," *Kansas Wheat Commission*, 2000, <http://www.kswheat.com/> (February 9, 2003).

2. "Kansas Salt Mine Warehouse Preserves Nation's Treasures," *The Morning Sun, Pittsburg, Kansas,* March 12, 2000, <http://www.morningsun.net/stories/031200/kan_0312000019.shtml> (February 9, 2003).

3. "Kansas Aviation History," *Wings Over Kansas*, 2002, <http://www.wingsoverkansas.com/history/> (September 18, 2002).

4. "A Brief History of Hillsboro Industries," *Hillsboro Industries*, Inc., n.d., <http://www.hillsboroindustries.com/company.htm> (June 17, 2003).

Chapter 4. Government

1. Kansas State Historical Society, "History of the First Territorial Capitol State Historic Site, *First Territorial Capitol, Kansas State Historical Society*, 2001, <http://www.kshs.org/places/firshist.htm> (September 18, 2002).

2. "Map of the 105 Counties in Kansas," *Kansas Association of Counties*, 1999, <http://www.kansascounties.org/kansas_county_map.htm> (September 18, 2002).

Chapter 5. History

1. Peter M. Chaitin, et. al., *Story of the Great American West* (Pleasantville, N.Y.: The Reader's Digest Association, Inc., 1977), p. 266.

Further Reading

Bjorklund, Ruth. *Kansas.* Tarrytown, N.Y.: Marshall Cavendish Corporation, 2000.

Connolly, Sean. *Amelia Earhart.* Chicago, Ill.: Heinemann Library, 2000.

Kavanagh, James. *Kansas Birds.* Blaine, Wash.: Waterford Press, Limited, 1999.

Kerkhoff, Blair. *A Century of Jayhawk Triumphs.* Lenexa, Kans.: Addax Publishing Group, 1997.

Kummer, Patricia. *Kansas.* Minnetonka, Minn.: Capstone Press, Inc., 2003.

Masters, Nancy Robinson. *Kansas.* Danbury, Conn.: Children's Press, 1999.

Netzley, Patricia D. *Kansas.* San Diego, Calif.: Greenhaven Press, Inc., 2003.

Sanford, William R. *The Chisholm Trail in American History.* Berkeley Heights, N.J.: Enslow Publishers, Inc., 2000.

Schultz, Randy. *Dwight D. Eisenhower: A MyReportLinks.com Book.* Berkeley Heights, N.J.: MyReportLinks.com Books, 2003.

Shannon, George. *Climbing Kansas Mountains.* New York: Aladdin, 1996.

Walker, Paul, Robert. *Great Figures of the Wild West.* New York: Facts on File, 1992.

Zeinert, Karen. *Tragic Prelude: Bleeding Kansas.* North Haven, Conn.: Shoe String Press, 2001.